THESE BLACK STARS

PAUL MURRAY

DEDALUS

The Dedalus Press
24 The Heath ~ Cypress Downs ~ Dublin 6W
Ireland

© Paul Murray and The Dedalus Press, 2003

Acknowledgements:
Thanks are due to the editors of the following publications in which some of the poems in this collection first appeared: *Céide, Cork Literary Review, Metre, Poetry Ireland Review, Cyphers* and *Spirituality*. "Eriugena in Old Age" first appeared in *Towards Harmony: A Tribute to Tony O'Malley* (Dedalus 1993)
The cover image : 'The Falling Stars', is from Hildegard of Bingen's *Illuminations*.

ISBN 1 904556 11 6 (paper)
ISBN 1 904556 12 4 (bound)

Dedalus Press books are represented and distributed in the U.S.A. and Canada by **Dufour Editions Ltd.**, P.O. Box 7, Chester Springs, Pennsylvania 19425
in the UK by **Central Books**, 99 Wallis Road, London E9 5LN

The Dedalus Press receives financial assistance from
An Chomhairle Ealaíon, The Arts Council, Ireland.

Printed in Dublin by The Johnswood Press

To my Mother

>Breath
>gone from your lips.
>
>Your hand in mine,
>a stilled branch.

To my Father

>The sound of your voice
>more faint than ever now
>
>still beating in my pulse
>like a tin drum in a dream.

Contents

Part One

In the Making	11
The Seagulls in the City	12
The Wall Fountain	14
The Gap	15
Eriugena in Old Age	16
Voice and Shadow	18
At the Edge	19
A Song for the Afflicted	20
The Sign	21
Death is No Stranger	22
Between	23
The Sun Tree	24

Part Two

The Witnesses	29
Insight	30
Invisible Storm	31
Lines for Natasha	32
The Delay	33
The Red Hand	34
Your Life	35
At the Year's End	36
A Journey Within	37
The Knowledge of Good and Evil	39
The Gift	40
Tell us, Poet	41
In the End	42

Part Three

The Second-Youngest	45
Days and Nights	47

Bewilderment	48
A Surprise	49
A Note in the Margin	50
What Remains	51
The Space Between	52
Meteor	53
The Breath, the Clay	54
Mind and Heart	56
The Shining Canto	57
Waiting on God	
(1) The Waiting	58
(2) O Sleeping Lord	58
(3) Invocation	59
(4) Song	59

Part Four

The Return	63
Night Wind	64
Hope	65
Stones and Stars	66
The Source	67
A Glance, A Word	68
Nocturnal	69
The Rock	70
Rising	71
Beginning	72

There are times of suffering which remain
in our lives like black absolutes, and are
not blotted out. Fortunate are those for whom
these black stars shed some sort of light.

Iris Murdoch

Part One

In the Making

The gift, when it comes,
comes always from where
you least expect: either

from that hurt void you feel
after actual loss
or from the mere absence

of a longed-for music,
from a line or a theme
you cannot seem to recall

or a phrase of a poem
you cannot complete.
But then with an instinct

born from that lack
or that need — suddenly,
out of the side

of the poem, another music
begins, another song.
And there it is on its feet,

bone of your bone and yet
free, flesh of your flesh
but not yours, a theme

like a new Eve emerging.

The Seagulls in the City

Bizarre
that you pursue me
this far out of the past,
                        arriving
in groups of two or three
on the wing,
          gliding
above the roof-tops,
and at all hours,
                   night and morning,
salting the air with your cries.

                    *

Useless
to pretend it could be different.
It cannot.
        For always
and almost against
my will
        something in my blood
wakens at the surprise of
your trespass,
                 something in my pulse
responds
to the strong, dream-like insistence
of your appearing.

                    *

At times it is enough
for me
        and for the earth-bound
if your wings tilt

```
downward
          even a little.
For in that instant,
              as the mind
turns on its axis and small wings
of desire
          begin to veer
back into the past,
it is as if the whole world
                    were tilting
sideways into the wind.
```

The Wall Fountain
(La Fontanella del Facchino, Rome.)

    Do not be surprised
if he is still there at the corner
of your thoughts, as once
    at the corner of your street:
the man of stone, that sad
exhausted man who leans out
    from the wall fountain
still holding in his marble hands
a barrel of stone that leaks
    water like time.
And do not be amazed
if you can still hear the sound
    that wakes in you
so many memories. Listen
and listen deep and well. Then
    let them pass.
For in or near this place
you love, this source, you cannot
    stop or trap the water
as it spills, or keep these days
and hours, these weeks and months
    from being poured away.

The Gap

I try, even now,
when the cold wind
blows through each sense

to close the door.

But hard though
I try, never have I
learned to hold firm

once and for all

the uneasy, loosening
hinge between
sense and thought.

Eriugena in Old Age

So many loops and bends has
this familiar path
it can still surprise me.

Sometimes it is like a
small child running up ahead
in the darkness.

*

But is it a path
that is real, this climbing path
that draws me away
from the most near and most visible:

my mind released,
as never before, by negation
of the obvious,
my five senses blurred

and the eyes and ears
of my soul enthralled,
as never before, by their perception
of the unseen and the unheard?

*

This climbing path, my mind's path,
now draws me away
from the care of this hour

and from the hub of a small world
of hours and minutes —
but is it a path that is real?

Voice and Shadow

Your voice at birth,
a gull-screech.

Your last breath,
the shadow of a sea-bird
on the vast waters.

At the Edge

No, there are no words,
there is no image to describe it,
the music of enchantment!

But, later, when the
notes of the song die out
one after another — 'the sweet cheat gone' —
what's left?
        Thoughts
at the edge of thought, hard-bitten,
crystalline.
          And no tremor
in the veins, no easy
rhythm of a woven music
                      but words
on the page, packed
with hurt and rapture.

A Song for the Afflicted

> *"To go to hell one need change neither one's place nor one's position."* — Rafael Alberti

This hell
has the sadness of pain
that cannot cry.

It is lodged
beneath the skin
beneath the mask.

It is a thing
that gnaws at being,
like a worm.

In this hell there is
no fire to feel, no flame
that stirs, no sound.

Yet — whose is that fire
within, that voice
which burns, and sings:

Hidden within the deepest
self — no matter how
treacherous one has been

or how corruptible — hidden
within the deepest self
the seed of love remains.

The Sign

    Yes, an uncommon hurt
though common in its source, a wounded
trust, an anguish felt for years.
    But what you have endured
of pain, the ways you have been
scarred, has etched a sign so deep
    it still appals.
Not the marks on a saint's body
those tiny, wounded stars
    on feet and hands
but the dark stigmata your name
and flesh received from the thongs
    and spears of rumour.
Sometimes I think
a brand on the forehead — like Cain's —
    would have been less cruel.

Death is no Stranger

To the living it is a well
of fear, a hidden
font of oil from which is fed
                              the flame
that burns
under all our thoughts, under all
our gestures.
              At times
it can appear like love itself
                            so real
as almost to keep us alive —
To the living, death is no stranger.

Between

Somehow it is enough, after
the day's long weariness of paths
and detours, if suddenly
                        a bird
calls in the stillness
and, between its clear
                        sharp summons
and your own heart, you hear
even the smallest silence.

The Sun Tree

Light, the last
of the light of day: look
at its branching form

how it spreads
like fire from the opposite
shore to where you stand,

a light so near you now,
so strong,
it draws your gaze

it lifts your thoughts up
into its branches,
into its nest of hope,

and holds you
there, and holds its ground
as if with shape

undimmed, with trunk
unbowed, it weighs
and flames against your loss.

Is it a sign? Is it
a blessing? You have not
asked for a sign

and there are no words
left. But blazing now,
and ending,

with all its myriad
leaves on fire, its wood
aflame, look how it dips

and sways on the water
as if, merely
by shining, to answer

the cold and the dark.

Part Two

The Witnesses

Already we had surged
    forward with the rest
        onto the bus

making it in just in time
    before the doors slammed
        shut behind us

but not in time to
    catch the stone
        brooch which sprang

from your dress and spun
    out through the doors
        like a tiny

stunned universe — all of us
    together on the bus
        staring after it

in amazement as if we were
    for that instant
        the astonished witnesses

of a first rock being hurled
    out into existence
        after the Big Bang!

Insight

As bright, as
sudden
      as the leap of
a grasshopper
            glimpsed
in a field of vision —

how swift
how extraordinary!

Invisible Storm

   It has not passed
through me, not yet, not passed
completely, the escaping
   tumult and its portent
still held within my senses.
What was it that loomed
   towards me? What
was it that appeared?
Something other
   than the rain, other
than the sound of the wind
coming in from the sea.
   But was I not
asleep, and wakened from
my sleep by the stirring
   of the sea wind
and the distant thunder?
And am I not
   remembering again
the first sharp breaking-in
of vision on my world,
   that storm
of hands at dusk, shaking
the huge and shining leaves?

Lines for Natasha

I will not bring flowers for your grave
not even the great lilies or the dark tulips
you loved.

I will not bring plaited wreaths or sermons
or even tears. The way you died has dried
all my tears.

I will not haunt your death.

I will not try to go back again
to the scorched room where you died
or to the thought of your fear at the end.

I will not seek
— not even for your sake — to re-live
the nightmare of the dropping flames.

I will not try to prove how swift
the end came, nor will I ask again
of your last seconds.

I will make no pact with your death.

I will not shape out of loss
or try to name the meaning of that hour
which had no exit.

I will make no pact with your death.

The Delay

    Now that the spectres
of the past, like rumours or like ghosts
of war, are drifting on every wind,
    how long must we await
your coming, Lord? Knowing so little,
destroyed by what we know, guessing
    so much and so much,
our lives, like the air itself around us,
woven with the threads of a story
    time alone can unravel.

    But you, Lord,
have you not signed the air
with your name, have you not carved it
    on our hearts with a comet's
god-like brilliancy and signature?
Why then do you remain
    remote from us, or why appear
so close yet indistinct, a radiance
unseen, a gift desired, a face, a name,
    our fingers trace in the dark?

    Now, even in our need,
when we try to pray to you, or try
to feed our minds on your presence,
    our thoughts are like words
in a dream, our prayers like crumbs
falling from the hand of sleep.
    Ah come, Lord, do not delay.
The weave and fabric of our lives
is worn: we need mending.
    Our righteousness is threadbare.

The Red Hand

When dreams are dipped
                  in blood
and words dressed up to kill
what does it matter
                which banner
or flag we carry
or what we're wearing — ritual
stole or sash?
            This anger
in our bones and blood, this hatred
on our tongue, is not
                the anger of God
but only hurt become dangerous.

Your Life

It may be over
the wind sang — over
before you know it.

Your whole life
blurred and shaken
as this hour
that stumbles on its feet
and flaps its wings
like a jackdaw —

Then lifts and is gone.

At the Year's End

Deliver from their
strange sadness, Lord,

those who are no longer
disturbed by love

and feel no fear, no pain,
as calmly, blandly,

they turn over the first
and last days of the year

like a coin in their pockets.

A Journey Within

As you enter,
the door swings back
against the light

behind you
and the world flashes
like a spent bulb.

Halted by the darkness
you are scarcely
able, at first,

to understand
where it is
you have come from

or why you are here
or where it is
you are going.

All that is clear
all that you can
understand

is that the
long lapse of time
has made you

a stranger.
And yet, even now,
even here

as the locked door
opens
into your emptied

memory, a small
trail of silvery dust
begins to stir.

The Knowledge of Good and Evil

1

The Apple

Almost mine —
but not mine yet.
              There it hangs
just out of reach.
            Ah, if only
I could grasp it, hold it
to my lips,
it would taste so delicious.

2

The Surprise

A windfall at last and no mistaking!
This is bliss, I thought, pure bliss.
I was so certain.
           Here, they said,
taste this, and again, taste this.
It is free, it is yours. Feast now
on a harvest of pleasure.

But what a sparse harvest it was,
what ghost sweetness!
From rind to core how sour
it was to taste that fallen fruit,
that unforbidden knowledge.

The Gift

Amazing —
no matter how
tired you feel
under the chill
downpour of
a dead routine
or how your
nerves and senses
ache, it's hard
not to affirm
the thought
that even under
the malign
powers of rust
and rain, the heart
survives, the soul
retains its gift
of weathering.

Tell us, Poet

    Tell us, poet, tell
us now, while the pulse of
colour still throbs
    in your idle veins,
what is the test of
love? How can we know
    if the dazed
instant, the moving circle
of enchantment
    on which we turn,
the moment's
live, unstoppable wheel,
    will burn out
under the weight of loss
or — under the force of
    love — burn on and on?

In the End

That they know it
or not, that we
know it or not
is not important.
What matters is
that all of us, all
of them, lovers
and madmen, mothers
and sad men — all
sing from a wound.

Part Three

The Second Youngest

My hair still dripping wet
after the bath and with, at last,
the large white towel which had
hung over my shoulders
now in his hands
I thought, as I knelt on the ground
before my father
and he dried my hair and talked,
I was the son of a god.

It was the same
warmth, the same repeated ritual
for all of us — my four brothers
and my three sisters —
when, in turn, after our bath
we would climb
the dark stairs to the lighted room
where my father sat in his chair.

We were, I suppose, like small
initiates: the girls
in their coloured night-gowns
and red slippers, and the boys
with our white towels
across our shoulders, wearing pyjamas
but naked from the waist up.

No pilgrims of the Absolute,
it's clear, no shining devotees
in saffron ever looked
as radiant and cleansed as we did

or ever climbed
to their illumined states of soul
as we climbed up those stairs!

I was five or at most
six years old, the second youngest.
But once I had
braved the darkness of the stairs
alone, my trial was over.
From shadows into light
the door opened, and I stepped
into the hush of the room.

So vivid, I remember, that bright
threshold! But real
illumination came, moments
later, when I knelt down
next to the fire, as near
as I could to my father's chair,
and bowed my head.

I remember, as soon
as he began to dry my hair
with the towel
and warm my hair with his hands
lifting his two palms
to the fire
and letting them rest on my head,

I thought I was the son of a god.

Days and Nights

All that's over now, you say,
all past and gone — and I agree.
    But wise men, wise women
of my generation, can you tell me
where they have gone, the days
    and nights of childhood,
where they are now? Have they
got lost within the loop of time?
    Are they in hiding?
Will they, if I learn their game,
if I take my hands away
    from my eyes, will they
come tumbling back from behind
the years? Wise men, wise women
    of my generation, tell me:
where are they now
the days and nights of childhood
    where have they gone?

Bewilderment

To the child's
first conscious gaze
or to the troubled seer

how utterly
wonderfully strange

the way time
loads our days with gifts,
with dangers —

how handsomely
it draws its fateful
circle around us.

A Surprise

    Scandalous,
no doubt, but a sign also
of a latent faithfulness
    in things

    and in us
of a surviving trust.
For though they blush
    scarlet

    with shame,
roses, clasped in the hand
or splayed in the arms of a hypocrite,
    remain beautiful.

A Note in the Margin

Amazing how
they seem to make sense
of us, though we

cannot
make sense of them,
those alarming

coincidences in our lives,
those rare
gestures of meaning

like twin
heads, facing each other
on the page,

eyeball to eyeball.

What Remains

If love is stronger
than death, will even
these, our pillaged

lives, our dreams,
one day be restored
like fragments

of a broken song?
Or will they
be changed under

some hand,
transformed like gathered
bits of wood

and coloured stone,
small fragments saved
from tumbled

walls we knew, from
stairs and vanished floors
and rooms?

The Space Between

> *I said: "God. I want freedom in salvation".*
> Arthur Rimbaud

What happened was for me
a kind of miracle

like being suddenly able
to breathe under water

the astonishment at finding
it possible again to believe

and at finding the space
to breathe and breathe deep

between the word 'freedom'
and the word 'God'.

Meteor

No matter
that it gleams, as
always, for a second

only, or for a
hundredth of a second,
the silent

meteor
of your glance, when it
passes near, recalls

a light
that shone from before
the beginning,

a radiance that broke upon
the stillness
like a wish formed.

The Breath, the Clay

  Unrecognisable
to anyone
but you, with your
  observant eye

  with your obsessive
love and craft,
the mystery we are,
  the actual mix

  of breath
and clay each one
is made of
  or made from.

  Our lives, our
loves, are mortal,
yes, but we are
  each one

  made in your
likeness. Our flesh,
our clay, formed
  in the unseen

  image of the
eternal Word, in the
dreamed likeness
  of the Son

      who would take
flesh. We are each one
formed in that image.
   Our spirit,

   the breath
in our souls and in
our lungs, like the breath
   of a god.

Mind and Heart

The mind
may hold to its aim
but who will

persuade the heart
of the mind's ideal,
its impossible

possible prayer:
never again to
lust after dreams

or to allow the
hurt of the past
unhinge

the real world?

The Shining Canto

Out of the night sky
a swarm of hiving stars
has entered my blood.

Their fallen light
has pierced me through
like a dying meteor.

Their alien
brilliance moves
along my veins

like fire.
They have burned
my lips and brow

so that I cannot sleep
for pleasure
in my blood

nor keep
a vigil now
unless that other

light, that nearer
fire, that other love
awakes.

Waiting on God

Four Songs for the Bride

> *"I sought Him whom my soul loves;*
> *I sought Him but found Him not".*
> The Song of Songs 3:1

(1) The Waiting

When, when will it come,
will it ever come, the moment
of ease, the arrested moment

when, through one urgent
wound of peace, your love
is known, your 'toil of grace',

and particle by particle
the fiery dust in my brain
begins to settle?

(2) O Sleeping Lord

If I could touch
my lips to this song
as to an icon

perhaps the pressure
of my lips
the music of my song

would wound your heart
and rouse you
from your sleep.

(3) Invocation

Like the flame that
survives until morning
and leaps upward

above the wood that it
consumes, may the spark
of this love survive

and may the flame
which absence kindles
not be put out.

(4) Song

So dark it was that night
when you came
near to me, so near

and with such love,
I could not find one word
to say but let fear

lean on love as you came
near, so near you came,
so near and with such love.

Part Four

The Return

    Still wondering if
the full spring will come
    but happy in the
knowledge my mind's dull
    winter has passed

here I am in its wake

    watching my
own thoughts fly in
    under the leaf
and shadow of a young
    idea, dipping and

swerving like swallows.

Night Wind

What is it
you are thinking of at night

when lying in your room
wide-awake

you can still hear though faintly
above the noise of the traffic

the night wind
coming in from the sea

whispering and humming to herself
like an ancient sorceress

and you know then
her burden of days is lifted

and the waves of the sea,
their hollows

filled with the night,
are at last beginning to ebb...

what is it you are thinking of?

Hope

Now, before the rains
prodigal of loneliness
and desire return, lift up
your eyes if you can,
raise them to the sun.
Let your thoughts
dare to imitate the swans,
those white birds you saw
lifting themselves up
noisily from the ponds
of childhood, and lean
with them, lean
as your hope lifts to the sun
far out into the wind.

Stones and Stars

    Always a cause
of wonder for me is how, after
hours of dull weather, days
    of drizzling rain,
that small cobble-stone street
outside my window not only
    begins at last
to breathe in the clear air, it also
somehow flames
    as it revives, changing
into a lane of tiny mirrors, a field
awash with light.
    Even now, believe me,
if you were to walk out
into the street at this hour, the wet
    cobble-stones
and the four or five yellow lamps
shining above them
    and the smaller lights,
all the lit windows of the houses,
would seem at once
    as wonderful a thing
as the sight of the thin lane of sky
over your head or as the thought
    of the infinite
dark, the vast firmament itself
sowed thick as a field with stars.

The Source

    Winds
out of the past are still
moving among the small
    grasses.

    And, nearby,
at the foot
of the Mournes, I can hear
    flowing

    out of the dark
earth, like a gift
restored, the quiet waters
    of the Shimna.

A Glance, A Word

Not always
will the stars feed
upon your blood

nor will
the clouds, as they pass,
starve

for your
eyes to transfix them.
There is

no need
to decipher the grammar
of past

and future. Here,
now, in your own
hands, and faster

than you can read,
the page of the moment
is burning.

Nocturnal

Under
their silence, under
their dark feathers,
                  birds,
a minor seraphim of
birds, a hive
            of tiny starlings
in a world of frost,
though sound asleep now
in the night's domain,
                        unmoving
in the icy cold,
            still keep
the notes of the song,
still hold
            the dream of the
warmth of the dawn,
                      under their
eyelids, under their closed
wings.

The Rock

First, it blocks your way
then opens it, an amazing,
improbable grace, but actual.

And the force of its weight
when it hits you — if
it hits you — marks you for life.

And there is no escape
from its hurt, though its force
weakens even as its weight

holds. And you are
struck so hard, at first,
and remain so stunned

that nothing in the world,
it seems, can protect you
from its curse: that jagged

fate, that rock
against which the heart's wave
rises, live and crystalline,

and falls
and breaks most powerfully
into the foam of the spirit.

Rising

Over the still
earth, the sun that
is rising now

is the sun
that was rising
before we were born

and will be rising
after we are dead.
And we, too, as it

dawns, revive. For
even as these
mists and fears

recede, shining now
above the dark
earth of the mind,

above the void,
three stars within us
rise, three

moving suns: passion,
wakefulness, joy.
And can such living

flame, such radiance
be born from dust
to return to dust?

Beginning

Now, after a long night
of stillness and longing,
on my brow, in the
tiny furrows of my palm,
thin lines of dew
are forming. And what I
had despaired of so long
is here. The sun,
true to its vow, with
prophecies of light and air
wakes the horizon.
I have come through
after all. I have a new
dawn on my shoulders.